Grace
for a time of sickness

Herbert O'Driscoll

Anglican Book Centre
Toronto, Canada

1995
Anglican Book Centre
600 Jarvis Street
Toronto, Ontario
M4Y 2J6

Canadian Cataloguing in Publication Data

O'Driscoll, Herbert, 1928–
    Grace : for a time of sickness

(Pastoral series)
ISBN 1-55126-134-0

1. Sick – Prayer-books and devotions – English.
I. Title.   II. Series: O'Driscoll, Herbert, 1928–
Pastoral series.

BV4910.O37 1995   242'.4   C95-932345-7

Glory to God,
whose power, working in us,
can do infinitely more
than we can ask or imagine.

Book of Alternative Services, page 557

Herbert O'Driscoll has written many popular books on Bible interpretation and Celtic spirituality. A well-known broadcaster and speaker, he has travelled widely throughout North America, Europe, and the Holy Land. In this series he explains, clearly and simply, what it means to be a Christian, and shows how Christianity enriches our everyday living.

Books in this series include

Birth: Holding Your Newborn Child
Baptism: Saying Yes to Being a Christian
Marriage: In the Christian Church
Eucharist: The Feast that Never Ends
Grace: For a Time of Sickness

For You

Chances are that you are reading these pages because you are experiencing a time of sickness. You are probably feeling some anxiety, perhaps even fear. It is very likely that you are also experiencing moments of loneliness. All in all, we can feel very vulnerable at times like this.

You need all the resources available to you during this time. You already have some—the skills of your doctor, the care of the nursing staff if you are in hospital, the care of someone who loves you if you are at home. If you live alone, there are friends available.

There can be other resources. Being a Christian means that you have access to a community of people who care about you. You might be surprised at the way in which church congregations today become communities capable of giving a great deal of care.

Finally, you have Christian faith itself. Don't worry if your faith seems rather weak right now. The important thing is that it is there deep within you—maybe forgotten, maybe neglected, but always there for such a time as this. It can be a wonderful source of encouragement, hope, and strength to you. These short pieces, based on some passages from the Bible, are an attempt to show you how Christian faith can be a most valuable gift at this time.

Blessings to you.

Herbert O'Driscoll

This group of readings from the Bible is based on a selection made on page 558 of one of the prayer books of the Church called *The Book of Alternative Services.* Other suggested passages of scripture can be found on page 587 of *The Book of Common Prayer.* Copies of both of these books can be found in most Anglican churches.

Isaiah 35:1-10

The wilderness and the dry land shall be glad, the desert shall rejoice and blossom; like the crocus

it shall blossom abundantly, and rejoice with joy and singing. The glory of Lebanon shall be given to it, the majesty of Carmel and Sharon. They shall see the glory of the LORD, the majesty of our God.

Strengthen the weak hands, and make firm the feeble knees.

Say to those who are of a fearful heart, 'Be strong, do not fear! Here is your God. He will come with vengeance, with terrible recompense. He will come and save you.'

Then the eyes of the blind shall be opened, and the ears of the deaf unstopped;

then the lame shall leap like a deer, and the tongue of the speechless sing for joy. For waters shall break forth in the wilderness, and streams in the desert;

the burning sand shall become a pool, and the thirsty ground springs of water; the haunt of jackals shall become a swamp, the grass shall become reeds and rushes.

A highway shall be there, and it shall be called the Holy Way; the unclean shall not travel on it, but it shall be for God's people; no traveler, not even fools, shall go astray.

No lion shall be there, nor shall any ravenous beast come up on it; they shall not be found there, but the redeemed shall walk there.

And the ransomed of the LORD shall return, and come to Zion with singing; everlasting joy shall be upon their heads; they shall obtain joy and gladness, and sorrow and sighing shall flee away.

Nothing is more beautiful than springtime in Israel, especially in Judea. The brown hills suddenly become a riot of spring flowers, all the more beautiful because their glory must surrender so quickly to the returning heat and dryness of summer.

As Isaiah knew well, this wilderness could be transformed each year. So can life itself, even if only for a short time. Into the wilderness of our illness can come moments of rejoicing. A caring conversation to a doctor can 'say to our fearful heart ... do not fear.' The arm of a friend visiting us can 'strengthen weak hands and make firm feeble knees.'

Illness, in an extraordinary way, can open our eyes and ears to things about ourselves that we have not wanted to see or hear. Then these things can be dealt with at last, and new possibilities can emerge in our lives like 'streams in the desert.'

An illness can lead us out onto a highway where life can continue. It may have to be lived differently. There may be new limitations we have to live with. But there will again be moments of 'joy and gladness' when 'sorrow and sighing will flee away.'

Isaiah 53:1-12

Who has believed what we have heard? And to whom has the arm of the LORD been revealed?

For he grew up before him like a young plant, and like a root out of dry ground; he had no form or majesty that we should look at him, nothing in his appearance that we should desire him.

He was despised and rejected by others; a man of suffering and acquainted with infirmity; and as one from whom others hide their faces he was despised, and we held him of no account.

Surely he has borne our infirmities and carried our diseases; yet we accounted him stricken, struck down by God, and afflicted.

But he was wounded for our transgressions, crushed for our iniquities; upon him was the punishment that made us whole, and by his bruises we are healed.

All we like sheep have gone astray; we have all turned to our own way, and the LORD has laid on him the iniquity of us all.

He was oppressed, and he was afflicted, yet he did not open his mouth; like a lamb that is led to the slaughter, and like a sheep that before its shearers is silent, so he did not open his mouth.

By a perversion of justice he was taken away. Who could have imagined his future? For he was cut off from the land of the living, stricken for the transgression of my people.

They made his grave with the wicked and his tomb with the rich, although he had done no violence, and there was no deceit in his mouth.

Yet it was the will of the LORD to crush him with pain.

When you make his life an offering for sin, he shall see his offspring, and shall prolong his days; through him the will of the LORD shall prosper.

In this passage, Isaiah is showing us a kind of portrait, although we will probably never know of whom. Christians think of Jesus as the subject in this portrait. Sometimes, especially in a time of illness, we will see something of ourselves in it. At such moments, this portrait can become a wonderful gift.

When we are wrestling with illness, our appearance can become very secondary to us. During the worst moments of illness, all we want is to survive, never mind how we look! We couldn't care less about such things. Then, as we gradually begin to feel better, and as we feel life returning, we once again reach for our soaps and creams.

In Isaiah's portrait, the sufferer feels rejected by other people. He feels 'as one from whom others hide their face.' We too can feel rejected during our sickness. We can be hurt by those who back away from us. It is as if they don't want to acknowledge sickness, even in a friend. Most often this is because they fear it in themselves. While this can disappoint us deeply, we need to try to forgive such neglect.

On the other hand, some friends can surprise us. In the lovely words of Isaiah, they 'bear our infirmities and carry our diseases.' They are present with love and support. Such friends can make all the difference.

In the Bible portrait, a wonderful thing happens to the sufferer—from anguish comes light. Our experience can be like this. Through this sickness, in itself so very unwelcome, can come new knowledge of ourselves for which we feel very much richer.

Isaiah 61:1-3

The spirit of the Lord GOD is upon me, because the LORD has anointed me; he has sent me to bring good news to the oppressed, to bind up the brokenhearted, to proclaim liberty to the captives, and release to the prisoners;

to proclaim the year of the LORD's favor, and the day of vengeance of our God; to comfort all who mourn;

to provide for those who mourn in Zion—to give them a garland instead of ashes, the oil of gladness instead of mourning, the mantle of praise instead of a faint spirit. They will be called oaks of righteousness, the planting of the LORD, to display his glory.

Sometimes it can be most effective to let certain statements linger and echo in our minds. We can say the words quietly to ourselves, several times, letting them sink into the depths of our being.

'The spirit of the Lord is upon me.' It doesn't matter what images we use to capture the meaning of this phrase, even though they may seem childish or foolish. What matters is that they convey to us the great and beautiful truth that the Spirit of God reaches out to touch our spirit. Then we realize that we have access to resources beyond our own.

'The Lord has anointed me.' Let the very sound of the word *anoint* flow into us. Remember the pleasure that oils have often brought to our skin.

Recall the touch of someone's hand. Think of that hand as the hand of God reaching out and touching us. When someone touches us during this time of sickness, let his or her hand be to us as the hand of God.

'The Lord has sent me.' Here in this passage, Isaiah feels sent to do many things—above all, to give the good news to his people, so that they will find their freedom. He feels sent to bring a joy and gladness that will energize them to build their country again.

For us there can be certain questions. What has God for me to do as I emerge from this illness? What joy and gladness can I bring to other lives? Who needs me to be energy for them, as my own energy returns? Is there someone who feels that their life has turned to ashes, and to whom I can offer a flame of friendship?

Wisdom 9:1 and 9-18

'O God of my ancestors and Lord of mercy, who have made all things by your word,

With you is wisdom, she who knows your works and was present when you made the world; she understands what is pleasing in your sight and what is right according to your commandments.

Send her forth from the holy heavens, and from the throne of your glory send her, that she may labor at my side, and that I may learn what is pleasing to you.

For she knows and understands all things, and she will guide me wisely in my actions and guard me with her glory.

Then my works will be acceptable, and I shall judge your people justly, and shall be worthy of the throne of my father.

For who can learn the counsel of God? Or who can discern what the Lord wills?

For the reasoning of mortals is worthless, and our designs are likely to fail;

for a perishable body weighs down the soul, and this earthy tent burdens the thoughtful mind.

We can hardly guess at what is on earth, and what is at hand we find with labor; but who has traced out what is in the heavens?

Who has learned your counsel, unless you have given wisdom and sent your holy spirit from on high?

This is a prayer first said by someone who lived nearly three thousand years ago. It shows us a picture. When we look at this picture, we are looking at God's infinite glory.

From out of that blazing light comes a beautiful woman. She appears as a figure of light, as if she is reflecting the light of God. Her name is Wisdom. Notice that her name is not Knowledge. Knowledge we can get for ourselves if we choose, but Wisdom comes to us as a gift of God. No wonder the person saying this prayer long ago wants very much to have this beautiful woman near.

We make the same request to her out of the same longing. At a time of sickness, we may find this longing very strong in us. We too ask Wisdom to come and 'labour at our side' that we 'may learn what is pleasing to you.' We know that 'she will guide us wisely in our actions and guard us with her glory.'

As we read this passage, we are being helped towards wisdom in our own lives. We need wisdom to recover from our illness. We need to know how to respond to all that is being done for us. We need wisdom to deal with the future, with the changes we may need to make in our habits and our daily patterns. To echo the words in the second last paragraph of this passage, we need the wisdom of God's Holy Spirit to set us on our right path on Earth, to learn what pleases God and allows us to live a fulfilled life from now on.

May this be so for us.

Psalm 23

The LORD is my shepherd, I shall not want.

He makes me lie down in green pastures; he leads me beside still waters;

he restores my soul. He leads me in right paths for his name's sake.

Even though I walk through the darkest valley, I fear no evil; for you are with me; your rod and your staff—they comfort me.

You prepare a table before me in the presence of my enemies; you anoint my head with oil; my cup overflows.

Ps. 23:6 Surely goodness and mercy shall follow me all the days of my life, and I shall dwell in the house of the LORD my whole life long.

To this day, one frequently sees shepherds in Israel. Sometimes they are boys, sometimes older men. They can be seen on the hillsides, seated by a herd or leading it into an encampment or chasing a wandering sheep or goat.

The image of the shepherd is probably the most vivid and lovely one we have ever been given to describe God's relationship with us. Within that image is care, nurture, gentleness, firmness, guidance, discipline, faithfulness.

It's interesting that these are the very qualities we would wish to receive from those who care for us in our illness. We will not find all of these qualities in any one person around us, but there will be those who embody some of them.

Guided by the language of the Psalm, let's take a journey. 'Green pastures'—places and moments of nourishment for the body and the spirit. When have we had such moments? 'Still waters'—moments of inner stillness, moments when we centre in the depths of our own being and sometimes encounter another with us. 'Right paths'—moments when we have a sense of progress, a sense of new direction, a glimpse of a way ahead.

'The valley of the shadow'—from which there sometimes seems to be no escape, especially in times of great loss, severe pain, heavy anxiety, deep depression. The Psalm speaks four words to us in this toughest part of the journey—God is with us. Say these four words again and again— 'God is with me'—until the realization slowly comes that goodness and mercy, a sense of belonging and home, can be found even in this valley.

Psalm 91

You who live in the shelter of the Most High, who abide in the shadow of the Almighty,

will say to the LORD, 'My refuge and my fortress; my God, in whom I trust.'

For he will deliver you from the snare of the fowler and from the deadly pestilence;

he will cover you with his pinions, and under his wings you will find refuge; his faithfulness is a shield and buckler.

You will not fear the terror of the night, or the arrow that flies by day,

or the pestilence that stalks in darkness, or the destruction that wastes at noonday.

A thousand may fall at your side, ten thousand at your right hand, but it will not come near you.

You will only look with your eyes and see the punishment of the wicked.

Because you have made the LORD your refuge, the Most High your dwelling place,

no evil shall befall you, no scourge come near your tent.

This magnificent Psalm does not for a moment deny the realities of life. It does not say that we can be guaranteed a life free from trouble, for even the deepest and strongest faith cannot provide that.

Within the Psalm, God says to us, 'When those who love me call to me, I will be with them in trouble.' The message of God to us is not that we will never know trouble, but that when we do so, God will be with us.

Listen to the words at the beginning of this Psalm—words like *shelter, shadow, refuge, fortress, trust*. Every one of these words refers to what God offers us at a time of need. These words speak of what God can be to us in a time of illness.

Again, the key phrases of this passage can form pictures in our minds. These in turn can flow into our feelings and then into our spirits. 'He will deliver you—he will cover you—under his wings you will find refuge.' Notice how the pictures are full of both strength and tenderness.

'You will not fear.' Let your lips form these words. Again and again. 'I will not fear ... I will not fear.' We can turn to these words in the dark hours of night, when we may encounter terrors that loom far larger than the realities that bring them to mind.

'He will command his angels concerning you.' As children we knew there were angels, messengers who communicated to us the messages of God. It is time now to allow our angels to return. They will come disguised as friends, as a family member, as a doctor or nurse or priest or pastoral caregiver. They will not have wings, but we will know that our angels have returned.

Psalm 103

Bless the LORD, O my soul, and all that is within me, bless his holy name.

Bless the LORD, O my soul, and do not forget all his benefits—

who forgives all your iniquity, who heals all your diseases,

who redeems your life from the Pit, who crowns you with steadfast love and mercy,

who satisfies you with good as long as you live so that your youth is renewed like the eagle's.

The LORD works vindication and justice for all who are oppressed.

He made known his ways to Moses, his acts to the people of Israel.

The LORD is merciful and gracious, slow to anger and abounding in steadfast love.

He will not always accuse, nor will he keep his anger forever.

This is a song of thanksgiving. We may feel like saying, 'I am ill. What is there to give thanks for?' But even in illness, there can be moments for giving thanks—for a new therapy, for a medication that has given some relief, for encouraging news, for the refreshing visit of someone whose presence means a great deal. At such times, there can be thanksgiving.

We are more in control of our thoughts and

feelings and responses to life than we often realize. We are not entirely in control, as we sometimes know only too well, but we are not without some control. We can decide to override our feelings and, as in this song, lift ourselves toward God in a moment of sheer, abandoned praise. To our surprise, we may discover that the act brings about the very reality we are seeking.

There is an arrangement of the hymn 'Amazing Grace' that has only two words, sung over and over. The two words are, 'Praise God.' That is exactly how this Psalm begins—'Bless the Lord, Bless the Lord, Bless the Lord.'

The song then moves into a list of God's grace or benefits to us. God forgives, God heals, God redeems, God crowns, God satisfies, God renews. Each one is joyfully said in such a way that grace is communicated from the spoken word to our listening spirit.

There is more. God's love is beyond calculation. God knows our most vulnerable humanity. Everything about our humanity is limited and transient. Everything of God is limitless. Bless the Lord!

Romans 8:18-25

I consider that the sufferings of this present time are not worth comparing with the glory about to be revealed to us.

For the creation waits with eager longing for the revealing of the children of God;

for the creation was subjected to futility, not of its own will but by the will of the one who subjected it, in hope

that the creation itself will be set free from its bondage to decay and will obtain the freedom of the glory of the children of God.

We know that the whole creation has been groaning in labor pains until now;

and not only the creation, but we ourselves, who have the first fruits of the Spirit, groan inwardly while we wait for adoption, the redemption of our bodies.

For in hope we were saved. Now hope that is seen is not hope. For who hopes for what is seen?

But if we hope for what we do not see, we wait for it with patience.

The letter that Paul wrote to the Christian community in Rome is his great effort to express what Christian faith meant for him. There has probably been more study of, and reflection on, this letter than any other piece of Christian writing.

But why do we find it offered to us at a time of illness? The answer is in one small but wonderful word—*hope*. These verses are one of the world's great expressions of hope.

Two things about hope are true for us. We cannot live our lives without it, and, especially in times of illness, the possession of hope can make all the difference in our capacity to recover.

Paul begins by acknowledging that the present time may be fraught with suffering, but he insists that the very nature of God means that something better is ahead for us. Life can indeed seem futile. Yet this very sense of futility is part of our human experience, because we sense deeply that it cannot be the whole story. We know that God's creation—of which we are a part—possesses a glory and a freedom far beyond the limitations and the frustration we experience.

Paul now returns to his theme of hope. 'In hope we are saved,' he says. Paul is saying that hope itself is an essential factor in bringing about the reality for which we hope. Hope is never pointless, no matter what the evidence seems to be. 'Hope,' says Saint Paul, 'hope for what we do not see.'

Romans 8:26-27

Likewise the Spirit helps us in our weakness; for we do not know how to pray as we ought, but that very Spirit intercedes with sighs too deep for words.

And God, who searches the heart, knows what is the mind of the Spirit, because the Spirit intercedes for the saints according to the will of God.

One of the demons that can attack us when we are ill, is our feeling that we are absolutely alone. It is not that people do not come to see us, although this can happen. Even those whom we hoped would support us, sometimes do not come. But sometimes, in spite of many people dropping in to see us, we feel deeply isolated. After all, we are sick while others are not. We feel that we are outside the ongoing stream of life, and we wonder—even sometimes fear—if we are ever going to be able to return to it.

The effect of this on our spiritual life may be the loss of our ability to pray. There is a demon within illness that can rob us of spiritual, as well as physical, energy. It seems to whisper to us, 'What is the use of praying? Maybe no one is listening.' When we couple this with the fact that anything remotely resembling a steady and disciplined prayer life is almost non-existent for most of us, we see why this can happen to us.

To say these things about prayer should not make us feel in the least guilty. Prayer can be difficult and elusive for even the finest and strongest Christians. Even great saints have agonized about the fragility of their prayer life.

To all of this Saint Paul says something wonderfully reassuring. First of all, he lifts any guilt we may have about prayer by saying, 'We (meaning all of us, not just you) do not know how to pray as we ought.' Then he offers something even more reassuring. 'The spirit helps us in our weakness,' he says. Then he goes on to say that the Spirit does our praying for us when we simply cannot, and with an intensity far beyond our capabilities.

These days we are fascinated by the self. We tend to think it the source of everything. But Christian faith tells us that above, below, and around the self is another and greater self. It is the 'self' or Spirit of God, who 'searches the heart and knows the mind' of my sometimes pathetic and self-centred self, who prays when I cannot, and who touches me with grace even when I cannot reach for it or bring myself to ask for it.

Romans 8:31b-35

What then are we to say about these things? If God is for us, who is against us?

He who did not withhold his own Son, but gave him up for all of us, will he not with him also give us everything else?

Who will bring any charge against God's elect? It is God who justifies.

Who is to condemn? It is Christ Jesus, who died, yes, who was raised, who is at the right hand of God, who indeed intercedes for us.

Who will separate us from the love of Christ? Will hardship, or distress, or persecution, or famine, or nakedness, or peril, or sword?

From all the encouraging words in the Bible, the opening sentence of this passage stands out magnificently. It is almost as if Saint Paul marches up to where we are in our sickness, takes us firmly by the shoulders, looks deep into our eyes, and says, 'If God is for us, who is against us?' Think of him as saying to us, 'If it is really true that God is our ally, then does it matter who is our enemy?'

Paul's measure of the generosity of God to our humanity—the degree to which God is for us—is the fact that we have been given God's most precious gift in Jesus.

If we look at the phrases Paul uses in the three

questions in the passage, we see a pattern of feelings we sometimes experience in sickness. There can be an overwhelming feeling that life itself is 'against us.' Paul replies that this may well be so. It is certainly true in sickness that certain elements of life are indeed against us. But God—ultimate loving reality—is for us. Therefore, there is far more *for* us than against us!

In a time of illness, we may feel that we are condemned to this suffering. We may even feel that it has come to us as a punishment for something we have done or failed to do. Again Paul lifts this from us. Our Lord himself actually intercedes for us, accepts us, forgives us, affirms us.

We can feel separated and cut off in our illness. In the face of this, Paul maintains with absolute confidence—and remember, he himself experienced much sickness, deprivation, and pain—that nothing, absolutely nothing, 'will separate us from the love of Christ.' Nothing!

Romans 8:37-39

No, in all these things we are more than conquerors through him who loved us.

For I am convinced that neither death, nor life, nor angels, nor rulers, nor things present, nor things to come, nor powers,

nor height, nor depth, nor anything else in all creation, will be able to separate us from the love of God in Christ Jesus our Lord.

In one of his letters, Saint Paul tells of his many sufferings. The list is appalling. He endures more than one shipwreck, is beaten at least five times, is thrown out of meetings, and is many times literally run out of town! To Paul, physical danger and pain are familiar friends. There are many times when he could well say, 'I am being killed all the day long ... accounted as a sheep to be slaughtered.'

Yet Paul has an extraordinary ability to find inner resources on such occasions. They enable him to conquer things that would otherwise destroy him. Where does he find these resources? If we could ask him, he would tell us that they come from his relationship with Jesus Christ as his Lord.

This has been his theme all through this part of his letter. Now, as he brings this subject to a close, he gives us one of the strongest and finest expressions of trust to be found in all his writings. Once again he hammers home his conviction that 'nothing can separate us from the love of God.' That love we experience through Jesus.

Having said this, Paul then ranges through the levels of human experience. Naturally, he does this in the language of his time. For him, the universe is a multi-levelled reality, reaching far above and far below things human. Time also stretches before and behind us. Paul ranges through the infinite context of human life, naming everything he can imagine. At the end of his list, he still maintains that nothing can separate us from the love of God in Christ.

We might use words different from those Paul uses, but we need to know the same thing. In spite of our limited trust, in spite of our sense of sometimes being forsaken and alone, we as twentieth-century Christians can know just as surely as a first-century Christian that we cannot ever be separated from the Christ who has bonded himself, by his infinite love, to every aspect of our humanity.

Romans 12:1-12

I appeal to you therefore, brothers and sisters, by the mercies of God, to present your bodies as a living sacrifice, holy and acceptable to God, which is your spiritual worship.

Do not be conformed to this world, but be transformed by the renewing of your minds, so that you may discern what is the will of God—what is good and acceptable and perfect.

For by the grace given to me I say to everyone among you not to think of yourself more highly than you ought to think, but to think with sober judgment, each according to the measure of faith that God has assigned.

For as in one body we have many members, and not all the members have the same function,

so we, who are many, are one body in Christ, and individually we are members one of another.

We have gifts that differ according to the grace given to us: prophecy, in proportion to faith;

ministry, in ministering; the teacher, in teaching;

the exhorter, in exhortation; the giver, in generosity; the leader, in diligence; the compassionate, in cheerfulness.

Let love be genuine; hate what is evil, hold fast to what is good;

love one another with mutual affection; outdo one another in showing honor.

Among the many therapies that have become popular in recent years, we frequently hear of such things as visualizing and imaging. Someone who is ill will be guided and encouraged to visualize that part of their body that is diseased, and to image it as healing or as already healed. At other times we may be encouraged to think of our body as a whole—the totality of our being as body, mind, and spirit—and to foster images of our recovery.

When we read the opening verses of this passage of the Bible, we realize how ancient such thinking is. While Saint Paul is not referring specifically to physical illness, he is encouraging us to develop attitudes in our lives that seek whole or healthy living in every way, including during our times of sickness.

'Present your bodies as a living sacrifice ... to God,' Paul tells us. We can immediately imagine opening ourselves to God, asking God to enter into us, or focusing on the fact that, as the source of all creation, God already inhabits the whole fabric of our being.

'Be transformed by the renewing of your mind.' Here Paul is saying that there really is a mysterious link between mind and body, a link that we in our Western culture are realizing again after a few centuries of denial.

'As in one body we have many members ... so we, being many, are one body in Christ.' Once again, although Paul is talking about Christian community, we can find helpful images as we read his words in our time of illness. Our body has many members and parts. As a total being, we are body, mind, and spirit. Yet these do not function as a machine. We are something much more wonderful—an organism. Health from one area of this being can flow to a diseased area. To know this and to practise this can lead us to our healing.

I Corinthians 1:18-25

For the message about the cross is foolishness to those who are perishing, but to us who are being saved it is the power of God.

For it is written, 'I will destroy the wisdom of the wise, and the discernment of the discerning I will thwart.'

Where is the one who is wise? Where is the scribe? Where is the debater of this age? Has not God made foolish the wisdom of the world?

For since, in the wisdom of God, the world did not know God through wisdom, God decided, through the foolishness of our proclamation, to save those who believe.

For Jews demand signs and Greeks desire wisdom,

but we proclaim Christ crucified, a stumbling block to Jews and foolishness to Gentiles,

but to those who are the called, both Jews and Greeks, Christ the power of God and the wisdom of God.

For God's foolishness is wiser than human wisdom, and God's weakness is stronger than human strength.

In the first Christian century, when Saint Paul was writing this letter, it was utterly incomprehensible to those from the surrounding culture how Christians could take, for the heart of their faith, a person who had been crucified as a common criminal. To be executed in this way robbed one of any respect and dignity. To hold up such a person as one to be followed seemed to be utter lunacy. To claim him as Lord and Saviour seemed beyond comprehension.

Yet Christians persevered. They insisted that the secret or mystery of the crucified God lay in the reversal of all preconceived human wisdom. They maintained that the wisdom of God stands human wisdom on its head and makes it look foolish.

As we read this passage during our time of sickness, we are being told that human wisdom is not necessarily the wisdom of God. Human wisdom, human medical skill, human logic, and human testing procedures may indicate many things to us, some that we do not wish to hear. To read this scripture is not to think we can dismiss or deny all such wisdom. That would be very foolish.

What this passage wishes us to realize is that medical wisdom, knowledge, and insight may not be the final word on our condition. Many other factors may come into play—not least of which is our own attitude and response, as well as the prayer and support of those who love us. Any experienced, wise doctor or nurse will tell us that they have seen utterly unexpected things happen in the face of perfectly correct diagnoses. Such things remind us how mysterious the body is. Body, mind, and spirit is ultimately beyond our human understanding. In the language of this scripture—the wisdom of God is greater than our wisdom.

Colossians 1:22-29

Christ has now reconciled in his fleshly body through death, so as to present you holy and blameless and irreproachable before God—

provided that you continue securely established and steadfast in the faith, without shifting from the hope promised by the gospel that you heard, which has been proclaimed to every creature under heaven. I, Paul, became a servant of this gospel.

I am now rejoicing in my sufferings for your sake, and in my flesh I am completing what is lacking in Christ's afflictions for the sake of his body, that is, the church.

I became its servant according to God's commission that was given to me for you, to make the word of God fully known,

the mystery that has been hidden throughout the ages and generations but has now been revealed to his saints.

To them God chose to make known how great among the Gentiles are the riches of the glory of this mystery, which is Christ in you, the hope of glory.

It is he whom we proclaim, warning everyone and teaching everyone in all wisdom, so that we may present everyone mature in Christ.

For this I toil and struggle with all the energy that he powerfully inspires within me.

As we read this passage, we are joining Saint Paul in a wonderful tribute to our Lord Jesus Christ. At this point, Paul tells us what Jesus has done for us by his death. He has taken our human nature in all its poverty and shortcomings, and by living this human nature perfectly—as you and I cannot do—he has removed the vast gulf between us and God. We can now regard Jesus as friend, companion, intimate. All he asks is that we remain faithful to him. From this faithfulness we receive the gift of hope, a gift that can make all the difference in times of sickness and suffering.

Paul now begins to talk about his own struggles. At the time of his writing, he is struggling to form Christian communities. Yet with Paul, the struggle is nothing less than a cause for rejoicing. He is so totally committed to his work that even the toughest challenges are a joy. Paul sees his struggle as a further contribution to the struggle of our Lord.

Reading this passage when we are ill takes us into the deep waters of Christian faith. Suffering in some form comes to all of us, but there are some great souls who have come to see and feel that their own suffering is their participation in that of our Lord. To do this is far from easy, yet to the rare souls who have entered into this mystery, a deep and rich meaning is given to what they have to endure. May our illness never be something meaningless. May it have a deep and rich meaning that enables us to respond to all that would heal us.

Hebrews 4:14-16

Since, then, we have a great high priest who has passed through the heavens, Jesus, the Son of God, let us hold fast to our confession.

For we do not have a high priest who is unable to sympathize with our weaknesses, but we have one who in every respect has been tested as we are, yet without sin.

Let us therefore approach the throne of grace with boldness, so that we may receive mercy and find grace to help in time of need.

In this short passage, we are at the heart of the really good news of Christian faith. The writer is using a vivid image from Jewish experience. Once every year, the High Priest would go into the Holy of Holies and approach the presence of God on behalf of the people. The writer suggests that we think of Jesus as our High Priest, but with one very important difference. Everything depends on how we think of Jesus and how we see his relationship to our own humanity.

At the heart of the Christian good news is the fact that God took our human nature, entered into it, and lived a fully human life. We see that taking, entering, and living in Jesus.

We have never been very good at understanding this. Perhaps it may sound too good to be true! Maybe a visualization would help. I close my eyes and imagine myself approaching the great throne of God. To say I feel utterly inadequate is an understatement. I feel utterly unworthy to be here. God has every reason to dismiss me from this blazing presence. But wait—who is here beside God? A figure I know, whom I have known ever since I was a child, a figure I have often forgotten, often betrayed, but one who has always been part of my life. As soon as I see him, I know there is someone here who knows my humanity because he himself lived it. Someone understands! Someone will help to have me accepted! Here is one who will 'sympathize with my weaknesses.' Why? Because Jesus 'in every respect has been tested as we are, yet without sin.'

Now I am able to approach God. Now I know that I can 'receive mercy and find grace to help in time of need.'

James 5:13-16

Are any among you suffering? They should pray. Are any cheerful? They should sing songs of praise.

Are any among you sick? They should call for the elders of the church and have them pray over them, anointing them with oil in the name of the Lord.

The prayer of faith will save the sick, and the Lord will raise them up; and anyone who has committed sins will be forgiven.

Therefore confess your sins to one another, and pray for one another, so that you may be healed. The prayer of the righteous is powerful and effective.

This letter of Saint James to the early Christians is often thought of as very practical and down to earth. It emphasizes doing and acting rather than just hearing God's word. As we would say these days, it is very 'hands on.'

How interesting then to read what James says about sickness. The very first thing he suggests is that we should reach out for help. We should reach out into the Christian community we are a part of and request that we may receive the laying on of hands with prayers for our healing. If we are not familiar with this, it can sound strange and even threatening. But in fact it can be beautiful and simple, and most important of all, it can be healing to us in ways beyond our knowing.

The reality is no more and no less than what we have said. One or two people whom we may or may not already know—naturally it is good if one or all of them are known to us—come to where we are. If our circumstances allow it, we may decide to go to them. We can meet with them in a quiet chapel, a living room, a hospital room. We may wish to kneel or stand or sit or lie, depending on our wishes and where we are. Hands are gently placed on our head, or, if we wish, on that part of us where our pain or our disease seems to be. One of those with us offers a simple spontaneous prayer at our request, naming our illness, offering us to our Creator as a body, mind, and spirit, and asking that the love of God may surround us, that God's healing may touch and enter us, and that the Holy Spirit—God's Spirit of wholeness, healing, and wellness—may enter the deepest levels of our being.

To experience such a moment is to feel supported by others, touched by care and love, and offered to a loving God. To experience this is to begin the work of healing.

Matthew 9:2-8

And just then some people were carrying a paralyzed man lying on a bed. When Jesus saw their faith, he said to the paralytic, 'Take heart, son; your sins are forgiven.'

Then some of the scribes said to themselves, 'This man is blaspheming.'

But Jesus, perceiving their thoughts, said, 'Why do you think evil in your hearts?

For which is easier, to say, 'Your sins are forgiven,' or to say, 'Stand up and walk'?

But so that you may know that the Son of Man has authority on earth to forgive sins' —he then said to the paralytic—'Stand up, take your bed and go to your home.'

And he stood up and went to his home.

When the crowds saw it, they were filled with awe, and they glorified God, who had given such authority to human beings.

Until recently, it was possible for us to be unaware of the fact that the world of the Bible—its very way of thinking about and looking at the whole creation—collided with the way in which Western culture had come to think.

In the Bible, creation is a seamless web of being, a whole creation. In recent centuries, Western thought tended to split creation into separate entities. The single example we have space for here, and the most relevant to this time of sickness in our lives, is that we tended to view our bodies as objects separate from our minds and our spirits, whereas the Bible regards these as a single reality, wonderfully and mysteriously linked together.

The very good news for us is that we have seen a return to this holistic way of understanding our humanity in recent decades. This new and, at the same time, very ancient understanding has begun to change many of our attitudes. We have come to realize that there are endless links between our thoughts, our feelings, and our bodies, and that our illnesses may often have their source in such things as anxiety, depression, and tension—just as these intangible states can in turn have their sources in the chemical imbalances of our bodies.

All of these insights are contained in Jesus' exchange with those around him. To the crowd, the acts of forgiving sins and healing limbs seem unconnected. Jesus knows otherwise. He seems to realize that unresolved guilt is somehow affecting this person physically.

The passage wants to tell us that sickness affects our whole being and that, as we reach out for physical healing, we might also ask ourselves if there are unresolved issues in our minds and hearts. To do this can open us to new levels of healing.

Matthew 11:25-30

At that time Jesus said, 'I thank you, Father, Lord of heaven and earth, because you have hidden these things from the wise and the intelligent and have revealed them to infants;
yes, Father, for such was your gracious will.
All things have been handed over to me by my Father; and no one knows the Son except the Father, and no one knows the Father except the Son and anyone to whom the Son chooses to reveal him.
Come to me, all you that are weary and are carrying heavy burdens, and I will give you rest.
Take my yoke upon you, and learn from me; for I am gentle and humble in heart, and you will find rest for your souls.
For my yoke is easy, and my burden is light.'

One of the most obvious things about our Lord Jesus is the intimacy of his relationship with God. He thought of God and constantly spoke of God as 'Father.' This relationship is obviously experienced by Jesus as one of great tenderness.

These verses contain a moment of such trust and tenderness. Notice how we are once again being reminded that, beyond our adult knowledge and intelligence, there lives what we tend to call, these days, the child within us.

Sometimes when we are ill, it can be wise to leave all the knowledge about our illness that we may have as an adult and, without apology, move to a child-like trust in a loving God. In such moments, we are acting out and responding to a great gift Jesus has given us. In his own love, he has shown us the love that dwells at the heart of creation; so we try to claim that love in our time of need.

Here, in some of the loveliest of all the words of Jesus, we are given an invitation. 'Come to me'—move from reliance on your own self to reliance on a greater self. 'You are weary'—carrying heavy burdens. You need to let go, not in a despairing way, but in a most positive and willing and hopeful way, so that as you acknowledge you cannot carry this load alone, you may regain the strength to carry it with God and, in time, walk free from this burden.

The yoke of life, especially in sickness, can become easier, and the burden of life can become lighter, when we allow our Lord to share it with us.

Mark 6:2 and 12-13

On the sabbath he began to teach in the synagogue, and many who heard him were astounded. They said, 'Where did this man get all this? What is this wisdom that has been given to him? What deeds of power are being done by his hands!

So they went out and proclaimed that all should repent.

They cast out many demons, and anointed with oil many who were sick and cured them.

When we read about 'unclean spirits,' we tend to think that we are hearing something from a world and a time very different from our own. In one sense, we are. In the world in which Jesus lived his earthly life, it was believed that much illness was the effect of evil spirits. Yet, if we think about our own attitudes to sickness, we begin to realize that we too have come to recognize that 'spirits' play a great part in our lives.

All of us know certain spirits only too well. They come to us at the most unlikely times. The spirit of anxiety, the spirit of fear, the spirit of guilt, the spirit of hopelessness. Sometimes they cross our inner landscape like a great shadow, colouring the way we see, feel, and react to everything. At such times, the very spirit we bring to living our lives is diminished and threatened. We function only partially as we try to keep going. We wait for the shadow to lift, sometimes trying to draw on our own resources, sometimes asking God for help.

There are even darker spirits, darker and stronger. They sweep over us, flooding our consciousness. They can be stronger experiences of those spirits already mentioned, or they can be spirits of utter despair and meaninglessness. This short passage gives us a piece of good news. It tells us that our Lord Jesus Christ has authority over such spirits.

There is an important factor in all this. To repent means to turn around. When dealing with the spirits that come over us, this may mean that we have to deal with things in our lives that we have tended to avoid. In this sense, we are being asked to do some turning around and, in this turning, come face to face with our Lord who is the Lord of our healing.

John 6:47-51

Very truly, I tell you, whoever believes has eternal life.

I am the bread of life.

Your ancestors ate the manna in the wilderness, and they died.

This is the bread that comes down from heaven, so that one may eat of it and not die.

I am the living bread that came down from heaven. Whoever eats of this bread will live forever; and the bread that I will give for the life of the world is my flesh.'

Sometimes we need to be reminded that even though our Lord's conversation with us is infinitely profound, it is also very simple and clear. Often it is we who have lost the ability to hear what he is saying and to trust his words.

If I believe that God lived out my human nature in Jesus Christ, I am also trusting that my personal life, in spite of all its shortcomings, is occupied by this divine presence. To possess such thoughts is to have the deepest possible sense of meaning about my life, a sense of meaning so strong that it is eternal. It just will not go away.

There are many ways in which we can think of the presence of God occupying our lives. Jesus himself gives us a wonderfully simple way. He says, 'Let me be the bread that you need to go on living. If you see yourself as eating this bread, as taking me inside yourself, then you will think of me as doing for your whole being what bread does for your body. You will receive me as energy for your soul. You will receive me as life itself.'

We can act out these thoughts during a time of sickness by asking to receive the bread and the wine of the Eucharist. This has other names you may have heard—Mass or Holy Communion. All of these names are an attempt to express what we believe about our Lord's gift of himself to us.

If you do not wish to do this, take into your hands a piece of bread from your next meal. Think of it as God's way of entering into your deepest being. Think of it as being handed to you by Jesus himself. Then eat it slowly and thoughtfully. Welcome the presence and the health and the life of Jesus into your body. Then say a silent thank you.